Systematic Guide to Reading and Writing Persian Language

Also by Mitra Ara

Eschatology in the Indo-Iranian Traditions:
The Genesis and Transformation of a Doctrine (2008)

A Lexicon of the Persian Language of Shiraz (2018)

Systematic Guide to
Reading and Writing
Persian Language

In Naskh & Nasta'liq Styles

by
Mitra Ara

Ibex Publishers,
Bethesda, Maryland

Systematic Guide to Reading and Writing Persian
In Naskh & Nasta'liq Styles

Copyright © 2018 Mitra Ara

Manufactured in the United States of America

The paper used in this book meets the minimum requirements of the American National Standard for Information Services—Permanence of Paper for Printed Library Materials, ANSI Z39.48–1984

Ibex Publishers strives to create books which are as complete and free of errors as possible. Please help us with future editions by reporting any errors or suggestions for improvement to the address below, or corrections@ibexpub.com

Ibex Publishers, Inc.
Post Office Box 30087
Bethesda, Maryland 20824 USA
Telephone: 301–718–8188
www.ibexpublishers.com

Library of Congress Cataloging-in-Publication Data

Names: Ara, Mitra author.
Title: A systematic guide to reading and writing Persian in naskh & nasta'liq styles / by Mitra Ara.
Description: Bethesda, Maryland : Ibex Publishers, 2017.
Identifiers: LCCN 2017043206 | ISBN 9781588141590 (hardcover : alk. paper)
Subjects: LCSH: Persian language--Writing. | Calligraphy, Persian--Technique.
Classification: LCC PK6228 .A73 2017 | DDC

Contents

Preface

Today, Persian is one of the major and most important languages of the Middle East. It is the national language of Afghanistan (in addition to Pashto), Iran, and Tajikistan, as well as the language of literature and religion in Asia Minor, Central and South Asia, and other regions. Up to the latter part of the nineteenth century, Persian was the literary and administrative lingua franca (that is, the language commonly used among speakers whose native languages were different) in the Indian sub-continent, and, therefore, is still a required language for its related studies.

Guidelines on learning how to write the New Persian language (also known as Fārsi, Dari, Hazāragi, and Tājiki) have thus far been presented concisely and often as an appendix to grammar books. This book, however, provides methodical, step-by-step instruction on the academic study of Persian writing and numerals as they are written and pronounced in standard form.

Persian is an Indo-European language, but uses a Semitic script with 32 letters which are fairly easy to learn. For practical purposes, I have included the names of the days of the week, seasons, and months as well. Students can use this book in self-study or in a classroom setting. I hope that this book will be of assistance to Persian language teachers as well.

The book also provides the necessary tools for individuals who are interested in studying non Persian languages that use the same Perso-Arabic or similar writing forms, such as Kashmiri, Pashto, Punjabi, Sindhi, Urdu, Uyghur, and others.

Introduction

This book is intended to serve as a manual and workbook for the writing system of the New Persian language, one of numerous known Iranian languages, in its Classical and Modern periods. This language, an Indo-European language similar to Latin and Greek, is distinguished from Old Persian, the language of the Achaemenid Empire (6th – 4th centuries B.C.E.), and Middle Persian, the language of the Parthian (3rd B.C.E. – 3rd C.E.) and Sasanian Dynasties (3rd – 7th centuries C.E.). Further, for the benefit of students, numerals, names of the days of the week, seasons, months, and transformation of Naskh to Nasta'liq writing styles are introduced.

Historically, the Old Persian language was mostly recorded in cuneiform script (from Latin "cuneus," meaning "wedge"), written from left to right and represented in inscriptions.

Cuneiform script inscribed on a tablet

Cuneiform script transcription

Middle Persian, also known as Pahlavi, evolved from the Aramaic script, and was written from right to left in Pahlavi script, as referenced in Zoroastrian religious books, Manichaean texts, and Sasanian inscriptions. The Avestan Zoroastrian script, also known as Din Dabiri, meaning "religious script" (in Middle Persian), was also developed and written from right to left for the purpose of recording the Avestan religious texts.

Pahlavi script

Avestan script

The **New Persian** language, as the third stage of Old Persian, is also a member of the Indo-Iranian language family, a branch of the larger Indo-European Family of Languages. As implied by its name "Persian" from the Old Persian "Pārsa" and the "Persis," as it was called by the Greeks, New Persian was originally a dialect of the province of Pārs (present day Fārs). New Persian "Pārsi," in its current form, emerged in the 9th – 10th century C.E., and became the lingua franca throughout Asia Minor, Central and South Asia, the non-Arab world, and the Islamic world. Note that the name Pārsi in South Asia also refers to Zoroastrian people of Persian origin who immigrated to India as early as the 9th century C.E. Today, the New Persian language and its writing system are globally recognized through the literary masterpieces of luminaries such as Hallaj, Razi, Avicenna, Ferdowsi, Attar, Ghazali, Omar Khayyam, Sa'di, Rumi, Hafez, and others.

Today, New Persian is the official language of Afghānistan (along with Pashto), Irān, and Tājikistan, and although it is not spoken as mother tongue in some regions, it is spoken by the majority in those countries, and is considered the national language.

The Pārsi (Persian) language came to be called **Fārsi** in New Persian only after the Arabic influence substituted /F/ for /P/ due to the lack of the /P/ consonant in the Arabic language. This resulted in Fārsi becoming the Arabic pronunciation of Pārsi.

The "endonym," meaning the name of the language as it is used by the people who speak it, may vary. For example, English is the name of language in its native land, but, elsewhere, it is called different names, for example, Anglais (French), Englisch (German), Inglese (Italian), Inglés (Spanish), and so on.

Similarly, Dari, Fārsi, Hazāragi, Pārsi, Tajiki, all being the same Persian language, are called Persian (English), Persane (French), Persisch (German), Persiano (Italian), Persa (Spanish), Pārsi (Persian), Fārsi (Arabic), and so on.

In Afghānistan, the standard Persian language is called Dari, Fārsi and Pārsi, and Hazāragi; in Irān, it is called Fārsi and Pārsi; and in Tājikistan, it is called Tājiki, Fārsi, and Dari. Similarly, the English language, as one language, is spoken and written differently as American English, Canadian English, British English, South African English, South Asian English, Australian English, and so on.

Accordingly, in maintaining uniformity with the names of other languages, the "Persian" language is called "Persian" in the English language. In this way, it is possible to preserve the richness and association of the language with Persian history, culture, literature, architecture, arts, music, food, and so on.

Development of New Persian script

The Persian alphabet, also known as Perso-Arabic, is a script made up of thirty-two letters, based on the twenty-eight letters of the Arabic alphabet. Adapted by Iranians over two centuries after the Arab Islamic conquest of Persia (7th century C.E.), it gradually replaced Middle Persian (Pahlavi) and other scripts.

The Perso-Arabic script is written from right to left in the same manner as Semitic languages like Arabic and Hebrew, are written. Students need to keep in mind that the Persian language is an Indo-European language, not a Semitic language, although it is written in a Semitic script.

The thirty-two letters of the Perso-Arabic alphabet are all consonants, except for one (alef), and contain four additional consonants (p پ / ch چ / zh ژ / g گ) not found in Arabic: /p/ as in **p**erfect; /ch/ as in **ch**oose; /zh/ pronounced /s/ as in mea**s**ure, and a /g/ sound as in the word bei**g**e, and, finally, the letter /g/ as in **g**ood. All the Persian letters are formed from eighteen characters and can be identified by the number of dots (1, 2, or 3) above or below the letter, or by the lack of dots.

Styles of Scripts

Several major styles of Perso-Arabic writing developed in Iran, out of which Naskh, Nasta'liq, and Shekasteh-Nasta'liq are the most commonly used. In this book, two universal forms of writing styles are introduced. First is the typeset style known as Naskh, meaning "copy," which is the customary form of writing for electronic media and print, and is primarily used for writing Arabic, Pashto, Persian, Punjabi, Kashmiri, Urdu, and several other languages. Second is a cursive-relaxed form of Naskh, like handwriting, called Nasta'liq. Because books, newspapers, computers, and websites use Naskh, students are encouraged to first learn Naskh before using other calligraphic styles, including Nasta'liq. There is also the Shekasteh style, meaning "broken," which is a shorthand writing style of Nasta'liq, with many different forms. Because Shekasteh-Nasta'liq is highly stylized and not used in language learning, it is not introduced here, but an example is given in the following pages. In learning the Persian language, Naskh and Nasta'liq are universally recognized as the standard forms for academic and general writing respectively.

Kufic Style

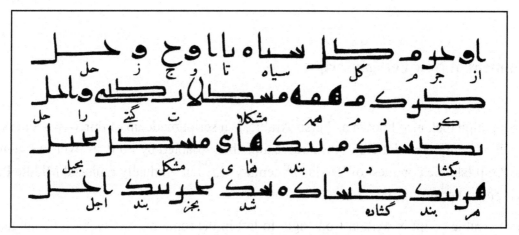

Kufic writing with New Persian transliteration

The Arabic writing system developed from the Aramaic and Syriac scripts in the 3rd – 4th centuries C.E., among the pre-Islamic Nabatean Arab tribes north of the Arabian Peninsula now present day Jordan. However, in order to preserve the Islamic holy book of Qur'an (Koran), early Muslims of the 7th century C.E. developed an incomplete form of current Arabic letters which gradually developed into the kufic style (named after the city of Kufah, Iraq), with angular and square-shaped letters devoid of dots, signs, and short vowel markings. Over the succeeding years, the writing continued to develop until the 8th century C.E., when Arabic writing developed into its current Naskh form. However, the kufic style continued to be used for writing the Qur'an, in decorative artworks, and the wall inscriptions of mosques and monuments.

Naskh Style

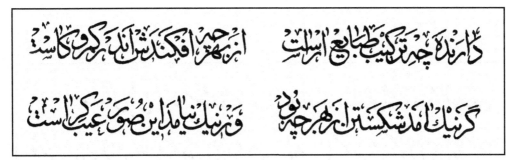

Quranic style Naskh, in Persian, with all the Arabic added markings

Based on the existing Kufic form, the Naskh style of writing, along with other forms, was invented by Ibn-Muqlah Shirazi (Iran, 9th – 10th century C.E.), an Iranian calligrapher. He is also recognized as the first to introduce calligraphy as a form of Islamic art. The Persian styles of writing have features and forms similar to Middle Persian Pahlavi and Avestan writings with round and curved outlines.

Standard Persian Naskh

Nasta'liq Style

Nasta'liq means "abrogated," as in abrogating or repealing previous forms of writing. A combination of the *Naskh* script and the Persian Ta'liq style, which was invented earlier by Hassan Farsi Kateb, based on existing Naskh and Raqa forms. Nasta'liq, invented by Mir Ali Tabrizi in Iran (Iran, 14th century C.E.), continued to be perfected by other Persian calligraphists through the 17th century C.E. as the predominant style used in calligraphy. In Iran, Nasta'liq became the most widely used script for artistic purposes, and is also practiced in Afghanistan, India, Iran, Pakistan, Turkey, and other regions for languages such as Azeri, Baluchi, Kashmiri, Kurdi, Lori, Persian, Punjabi, Sindhi, Urdu, and others. Because of its flexibility and aesthetic value, the *Nasta'liq* style is frequently used for everyday handwriting. Personal letters, important messages, signs, poems, and decorative writings are also often written in this style (see section on Transformation of Naskh to Nasta'liq).

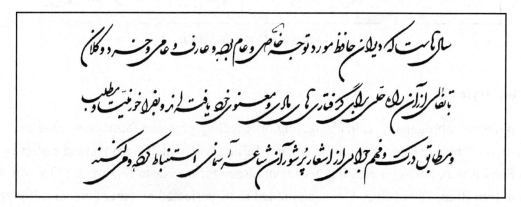

Persian Nasta'liq

Shekasteh Nasta'liq Style

The later creation of Shekasteh Nasta'liq, meaning "broken" Nasta'liq, is attributed to Mirza Muhammad Shafi (Iran, 17th century C.E.). This ornamental style of writing is generally used by calligraphists only and not used for basic writing.

Persian Shekasteh Nasta'liq

Persian Script and Pronunciation

Learning the Persian alefbā (**alphabet**), including the 32 letters, vowels, diphthongs, signs, and their cursive forms (connected forms), is essential prior to embarking on grammar lessons.

Students may initially find Persian writing complex due to its cursive appearance, but it can be easily learned following the instructions in this book.

The Persian alphabet provides graphic representations only for the long vowels (ā, ī, ū) and for the diphthongs (āy, ey/eī, ow, oy, and uy). Because Persian is a consonantal system, the short vowels (a, e, o) do not have a letter representation and may or may not be marked, depending on the nature of the text. Other languages, such as English, also do not distinguish certain sounds. For example, in English, there is no written distinction between English short and long vowels, such as the short /a/ in "bat" as opposed to the long /ā/ in "tall."

Diacritics, which are signs placed above and below letters indicating different sounds, are used in marking short vowels above and below the letters, as well as marking other signs. In this book, long vowels in English are also marked with a line over the letter, which typically would have a different sound, such as short vowels /a, e, o/ contrasted with long vowels /ā, ī, ū/.

In everyday reading and writing, short vowels are often not marked. In order to learn the language, however, they may be marked until the pronunciation of the word is recognized and memorized. This will become clearer through the examples appearing in the pertinent section of this book.

- The Perso-Arabic script is written from right to left following the manner in which Semitic languages, including Arabic and Hebrew, are written.

- Of course, the Persian language is an Indo-European language, not a Semitic language, although it is written in a Semitic script.

- As indicated before, it is useful to first learn the alphabet in the Naskh style, which is used in all printed materials.

- In Naskh, the letters are either in their full form or in shortened form. The shortened form is used in the initial-joined (joined on the left) and medial-joined (joined on both sides) positions.

- The full forms are used in the isolated/alone/non-connected and final-joined (joined on the right) positions.

- Keep in mind that there is no capitalization in Persian writing.

- As in English, the handwritten letters appear slightly different from the typeset, and different fonts provide different stylistic forms. Nonetheless, the integrity of the form of the letters and the sounds should not be affected.

Ligature

The letters are connected to the preceding and following letter by a short ligature, a connected line about a hyphen length (-). Ligatures may alter the shape of the letters, so that, in grouping, some letters may appear to have changed their form entirely, particularly if the diacritic points (dots, signs, and short vowels) are sloppily positioned.

Dots

In the case of the letters sharing the same appearance, a dot or dots are used to distinguish them phonetically from one another.

- A combination of one, two, and three dots are positioned centered-above or centered-below a group of letters.

- It is important that each dot is accounted for and positioned accurately as each dot provides a phonetic marking for each letter.

- First, write the body of the letter, and, second, place the dots.

- Examples of dot formation and position:

ب پ ت ث

ج چ خ

ذ ز ژ

ش ض ظ

غ ف ق ن

Letters of the Alphabet

In the following chart, the Persian letters are listed in the order as they appear in most modern dictionaries.

- The chart shows the possible positions and forms of the letters, their Persian names, and their phonetic transcription.

- Certain letters, marked as non-connectors (**nc**) in the list below, join on the right only.

- Letters which are uniquely Persian and thus not found in Arabic are marked with an asterisk (*).

- When joined together in words, most of the letters modify their outlines to the extent of dropping any tail or belly they may possess in their unconnected form.

Persian alphabet chart

Sound represented	Name	Letter			
			Joined		
		isolated	to the preceding	from the two sides	to the following letter
no sound (see vowels)	alef (nc)	ﺍ (nc)	ﻝ	-	-
b as in boy	be	ﺏ	ﺐ	ﺒ	ﺑ
p as in pen	pe*	ﭖ*	ﭗ	ﭙ	ﭘ
t as in tell	te	ﺕ	ﺖ	ﺘ	ﺗ
s as in sell	se	ﺙ	ﺚ	ﺜ	ﺛ
j as in joy	jim	ﺝ	ﺞ	ﺠ	ﺟ
ch as in cheese	che*	ﭺ*	ﭻ	ﭽ	ﭼ

h as in house	he-jimi/ he-hotti	ح	ح	ح	ح
kh as "ch" in German Bach	khe	خ	خ	خ	خ
d as in doll	dāl (nc)	د (nc)	ـد	ـد	د
z as in zoo	zāl (nc)	ذ (nc)	ـذ	ـذ	ذ
r as in rest	re (nc)	ر (nc)	ـر	ـر	ر
z as in zoo	ze (nc)	ز (nc)	ـز	ـز	ز
zh as 'g' in beige	zhe (nc)*	ژ (nc)*	ـژ	ـژ	ژ
s as in sun	sin	س	ـس	ـسـ	سـ
sh as in shine	shin	ش	ـش	ـشـ	شـ
s as in sun	sād	ص	ـص	ـصـ	صـ
z as in zoo	zād	ض	ـض	ـضـ	ضـ
t as in tell	tā	ط	ـط	ـطـ	طـ
z as in zoo	zā	ظ	ـظ	ـظـ	ظـ
a as in ant	'eyn	ع	ـع	ـعـ	عـ
q as "r" in French merci	qeyn	غ	ـغ	ـغـ	غـ
f as in fox	fe	ف	ـف	ـفـ	فـ
q as "r" in French merci	qāf	ق	ـق	ـقـ	قـ
k as in keep	kāf	ک	ـک	ـکـ	کـ

g as in good	gāf*	گ*	ـگ	ـگـ	گـ
l as in love	lām	ل	ـل	ـلـ	لـ
m as in mine	mim	م	ـم	ـمـ	مـ
n as in name	nun	ن	ـن	ـنـ	نـ
v as in vote, o in more, oo/u in moose, w in water	vāv (nc)	و (nc)	ـو	ـو	و
h as in honey (real he) h as in honor (silent he)	he-havvaz/ du-chashm (two-eyed)	ه	ـه	ـهـ/ـه	ه/ﻫ
y as in yes i as in film	ye	ی	ـی	ـیـ	یـ

* Persian letters not found in Arabic.

(nc) Non-connectors connect only to the preceding letter and never to the following letter.

Non-connectors (nc)

There are seven letters, plus long vowel /ā/, marked as non-connectors (**nc**); that is, they do not connect to the following letter, but they do connect to the letter before them in the medial and final positions:

- Alef / ا / in the initial position, functioning only as the bearer of the short vowels:

$$a\ \overline{ا}\ /\ e\ \underline{ا}\ /\ o\ \overset{\circ}{ا}$$

- Alef-madde, **ā** / آ /, as in the word m**a**ll, is an alef with a tilde-hat (~), functioning as a long vowel **ā** in all positions (it loses its hat in the middle and final positions).

- At this stage, students should not concern themselves with learning the vowels until they first learn the consonants.

- Consonants:

d	د
z	ذ
r	ر
z	ز
zh	ژ
v	و

Similarly shaped letters

Varied form	Full form
بـ پـ تـ ثـ / نـ / يـ	ب / ن / ی
جـ چـ حـ خـ	ح
د ذ	د
ر ز ژ	ر
سـ شـ	س
صـ ضـ	ص
طـ ظـ	ط
عـ ـعـ / غـ ـغـ	ع
ـف / ـق	ف / ق
کـ گـ / ـل	ک / ل

Multiple letters with one sound

In Persian, as in English, a single sound corresponds to several letters, such as the sound /k/ in the words **c**at, **k**ale, **q**uick, and **Sch**edule (American English pronunciation).

In Persian, the eight letters / ق q / ع ' / ظ z / ط t / ض z / ص s / ح h / ث s / are generally found in Arabic loan words, and / ق / ط / ص / in Turkish words as well. Because their Arabic sounds are not found in Persian, their pronunciations have been modified to Persian sounds.

- Consequently, these eight consonants, in bold, represent the same sounds as their Persian corresponding sounds.

t	ت ط
s	ث س ص
z	ذ ز ض ظ
h	ح ه
(sounds like a hiatus, stop)	ء ع
q	غ ق

Multiple sounds with one letter

In Persian, as in English, a letter may have more than one sound, such as the English letter /c/ in the word **c**andy (pronounced as kandy), in **c**ity (pronounced as sity), in deli**c**ious (pronounced as delishous), or not pronounced in the word s**c**ience (pronounced as sience).

In Persian, the letters /vāv و/ and /he-havvaz ه/ are presented in one form but have multiple sounds. Due to the complexity of their usages, they are introduced in the subsequent lessons after the consonants and vowels are practiced (see section on Various Sounds of the Same Letter).

Begin to Write the Letters

By now you have studied the alphabet chart and have familiarized yourself with the letters and pronunciations.

- Begin your writing practices using a lined paper and pencil instead of an ink pen because you may need to erase and revise several times in order to perfect the shape of each letter.

- Lines on the paper guide you to write in a straight line and avoid writing up and downhill. They also help you determine the right size and proportion for each letter, important because you need to determine that each connected form, when a letter follows, is half the size of its full final position and alone form. Just as in English, each lower case/connected letter is smaller than its capital form, such as /s/ being half the size of its uppercase alone /S/.

- Keep in mind that, in Persian writing, there are no capitalizations, only shortened and full forms.

- Writing from right to left, move your pencil in the direction shown by the arrow with respect to the horizontal line on the paper.

- Remember to use a ligature (a slur or tie) when connecting to the following letter.

- First draw the body of the letter, then mark the tilde, strokes and handles, then carefully mark the dot(s) where they belong (if any), paying close attention to the position and number of dots, then mark the short vowels, and, lastly, mark the signs.

Group 1

This group contains only one letter, the first letter of the alphabet, called /**alef**/.

• As a non-connector, this letter by itself does not have any sound or function, and is neither a consonant nor a vowel.

Name	Isolated	Final	Medial	Initial
alef	.........ا.........	-	-	.........ا.........

	....	....	....	....
	....	....	....	....
	....	....	....	....
	....	....	....	....

- However, /alef/ is used as a vessel, or bearer, for initial short vowels (**a, e, o**), (see Vowels).

Pronounciation	Initial
a (**adam**)	آ
e (**enter**)	اِ
o (**toy**)	اُ

- Alef is also used for forming the long vowel /ā/ as in /b**a**ll/. In the initial position, the long vowel /ā/ is marked by a hat, like the tilde symbol (~), placed over the alef /آ/. The sign is called "maddah" in Arabic, meaning "lengthening."

- The same long vowel (in Persian, **alef-madd**) in the medial and final positions graphically loses the hat, but the /alef/ is still pronounced as a long /ā/.

Group 2

This group contains / **be** / **pe** / **te** / **se** /.

- They are all connectors and therefore appear in all positions: isolated (non-connected) and joined (initial, medial, and final).

- These letters all share the same basic graphic forms, and the only marker that determines their particular sound and function is the number of dots positioned above and below each letter.

- Consequently, it is extremely important that the dot(s) are marked legibly, otherwise they can be misread. Pay close attention to the formation and positioning of the dots below and above each letter.

- In their initial and medial positions, the letters are written as two-thirds shorter, with the dots placed center below and center above each letter, respectively (also see groups 14 and 17).

- The initial and medial forms of the letters /nun ن/ and /ye ی/ are formed in the same way, only with differences in the positioning of the dots.

- There are other letters with different forms sharing the exact sound as /te/ and /se/ (see section on Multiple letters with one sound).

- First draw the body of the letter, then mark the dots.

Name & Pronunciation	Isolated	Final	Medial	Initial
be (**b**ell)	.......ب.......	.....بـ.....ـبـ.....	.......ـبـ.......	.......بـ.......
ب	....	....	....	....
	....	....	....	....
	....	....	....	....
	....	....	....	....

Name & Pronunciation	Isolated	Final	Medial	Initial
pe (pen)	پ	ـپ	ـپـ	پـ
پ				

Name & Pronunciation	Isolated	Final	Medial	Initial
te (**t**all)	.......ت.......	.......ـت.....	........ـتـ........	.......تـ........
ت	....	....	....	....
	....	....	....	....
	....	....	....	....
	....	....	....	....

Name & Pronunciation	Isolated	Final	Medial	Initial
se (side)	........ث.......	.....ـث....	...ـثـ.....	....ثـ....
ث	....	....	....	....
	....	....	....	....
	....	....	....	....
	....	....	....	....

Group 3

This group contains /**jim/che/he-jimi/khe**/.

- This /he-jimi/ is also called /he-hotti/ and is discernable from the other /he/ (he-havvaz), which will be introduced later, in group 16. In Persian, contrary to Arabic, both /he/ forms are pronounced the same.

- Pay closer attention to the placing of the dot(s) below each letter in their different positions. In their isolated and final positions, the dots are placed at the center of the belly, but, in their initial and medial positions, their belly is lost and the dots are placed center below and above the head, respectively.

- The letter /**khe**/ has a similar sound as the letter /**ch**/ in German name Ba**ch**. It has a scraping sound that is created in the back of the throat, as one would try to clear the throat.

- First draw the body of the letter, then mark the dots.

Name & Pronunciation	Isolated	Final	Medial	Initial
jim (jar)	····· ح ·····	····· ح ····	····· ح ····	····· ح ·····
		·················	·················	·················	·················
		·················	·················	·················	·················
		·················	·················	·················	·················
		·················	·················	·················	·················

Name & Pronunciation	Isolated	Final	Medial	Initial
che (mu**ch**)	چ	چـ	ـچـ	چـ

چ	....	....	....	....
	....	....	....	....
	....	....	....	....
	....	....	....	....

Name & Pronunciation	Isolated	Final	Medial	Initial
he (**h**at)	ح	حـ	ـحـ	حـ

Name & Pronunciation	Isolated	Final	Medial	Initial
khe as in German (Ba**ch**)	خ	ـخ	ـخـ	خـ

	....	....	....	....
	....	....	....	....
	....	....	....	....
	....	....	....	....

Group 4

This group contains /**dāl**/**zāl**/ non-connectors, similar to group one.

- The letter /zāl/ is mostly found in Arabic words. Pay close attention to the placing of the one dot directly over the letter.

Name & Pronunciation	Isolated	Final	Medial	Initial
dāl (**deep**)	.........ﺩ.........	........ﺪ......	......ﺪ......	.........ﺩ........
	....	....	....	....
	....	....	....	....
	....	....	....	....
	....	....	....	....

Name & Pronunciation	Isolated	Final	Medial	Initial
zāl (zebra)	........ذ........	......ـذ......	......ـذـ......	........ذ........
ذ	....	....	....	....
	....	....	....	....
	....	....	....	....
	....	....	....	....

Group 5

This group contains **/re/ze/zhe/** non-connectors, similar to group 1 and 4.

- Pay close attention to the number and placing of the dots directly over the letters /ze/zhe/.

- The letter /zhe/ sounds like the letter /s/ as in measure, and a /g/ sound in the words beige, mirage, garage, and borage.

Name & Pronunciation	Isolated	Final	Medial	Initial
re (root)	....ر....	....ر....	....ر....	....ر....
	....	....	....	....
	....	....	....	....
	....	....	....	....
	....	....	....	....

Name & Pronunciation	Isolated	Final	Medial	Initial
ze (**z**ero)	.......ز.......	.......ـز.......	.......ـزـ.......	.......ز.......
ز	....	....	....	....
	....	....	....	....
	....	....	....	....
	....	....	....	....

Name & Pronunciation	Isolated	Final	Medial	Initial
zhe (measure)	ژ	ـژ	ـژ	ژ
ژ				

Group 6

This group includes /**sin**/**shin**/, written by three teeth.

- In initial and medial positions the belly is eliminated.

- Pay close attention to the placing of the three dots at the center and over the teeth of the letter /shin/.

Name & Pronunciation	Isolated	Final	Medial	Initial
sin (summer)	......سـ......	......ـس....	........ـسـ.....	.......سـ.......
	....	....	....	....
	....	....	....	....
	....	....	....	....
	....	....	....	....

Name & Pronunciation	Isolated	Final	Medial	Initial
shin (**shy**)	......ش......	.....ش.....	......ش......	......ش......
ش	....	....	....	....
	....	....	....	....
	....	....	....	....
	....	....	....	....

Group 7

This group includes /**sād/zād**/, both letters found only in Arabic words.

- In their initial and medial joined forms, the belly is eliminated and they gain a tooth, after which another letter may be connected.

- Pay attention to the placing of one dot at the center and over the head of the letter /zād/.

Name & Pronunciation	Isolated	Final	Medial	Initial
sād (soon)	......ص......	......ص......	......ص......	......ص......
ص	....	....	....	....
	....	....	....	....
	....	....	....	....
	....	....	....	....

Name & Pronunciation	Isolated	Final	Medial	Initial
zād (zoo)	......ض......	......ض......	......ض......	......ض......
ض	....	....	....	....
	....	....	....	....
	....	....	....	....
	....	....	....	....

Group 8

This group includes /**tā/zā**/, both letters found in Arabic words.

- In writing these letters, the handle, the vertical line, must be placed after the head is formed.

- Writing this letter requires two strokes, head first and then the handle.

- This is similar to placing the dots after the main body of the letter is formed. Here, in the case of /zā/, first form the head of the letter, second draw the handle to connect with the head, and, third, place one dot centered over the head.

Name & Pronunciation	Isolated	Final	Medial	Initial
tā (type)	........ﻂ.......	.....ﻂ........	.....ﻂ.....	......ﺑ.......
	....	....	....	....
	....	....	....	....
	....	....	....	....
	....	....	....	....

•

Name & Pronunciation	Isolated	Final	Medial	Initial
zā (zen)	ظ	ظ	ظ	ظ
ظ	....	....	....	....
	....	....	....	....
	....	....	....	....
	....	....	....	....

Group 9

This group includes /**eyn**/**qeyn**/ letters. The former is found in Arabic words, but the latter is used in some Persian words as well as Arabic and Turkish.

- In English translation, /eyn/ with a glottal stop sound is marked as an apostrophe /ʿ/ or an open quotation mark /ʿ/.

- The sound /eyn/ is like the stop of /**a**/ in the word **ant**, or the stop between the syllabus of "uh oh."

- The sound of the letter /qeyn/ is not found in English. It is similar to the gobbling sound of a turkey, transliterated with the letter /q/.

- In their initial and medial positions the tail is eliminated.

- Pay close attention to the placing of a dot at the center and over the head of the /qeyn/ in all positions.

Name & Pronunciation	Isolated	Final	Medial	Initial
eyn (as the stop in the middle of uh-uh)	ع	ح	ـع	ع

Name & Pronunciation	Isolated	Final	Medial	Initial
q (in French merci)	غ	ـغ	ـغـ	غـ
غ / غ				

Group 10

This group includes /**fe**/**qāf**/, with the latter transliterated with the letter /q/, similar to the letter /qeyn/.

- The sound of /qāf/ does not occur in English. It shares the same turkey gobbling sound as the letter /qeyn/ in group 9. It also sounds like the letter /**r**/ in French word merci.

- In forming the round-shaped head of these two letters, pay close attention to clearly marking the dots at the center and over the round head, with one dot for the letter /fe/ and two dots for /qāf/; otherwise, they appear the same and can be misread.

Name & Pronunciation	Isolated	Final	Medial	Initial
fe (form)	......ف......	....ـف....	......ـفـ......	......ف........
ف	....	....	....	....
	....	....	....	....
	....	....	....	....
	....	....	....	....

Name & Pronunciation	Isolated	Final	Medial	Initial
q (as in French me**r**ci)	.......ق........	.......ﻖ......	......ﻘ........	......ﻗ........
ﻗ	....	....	....	....
	....	....	....	....
	....	....	....	....
	....	....	....	....

Group 11

This group contains /**kāf/gāf**/. In writing these two letters, the slanted strokes, placed over the body of the letters, connect to the handles.

- In the case of /gāf/, an additional shorter stroke is placed at the center above the lower longer stroke.

- All strokes are made after the main body is first formed. The entire letter, including the strokes, should not be written in one stroke.

- If these two letters are positioned before /alef/ (group 1) and /lām/ (group 12), their graphic forms change (see section on Orthographic of connected combinations).

- Note that the Arabic writing form of the letter ke /ﻙ ﻜ / in the final and isolated positions changes to /ﻚ ﻜ /.

Name & Pronunciation	Isolated	Final	Medial	Initial
kāf (book)	......ﻙ........	...ﻚ.....	......ﻜ........	....ﻛ........
	....	....	....	....
	....	....	....	....
	....	....	....	....
	....	....	....	....

Name & Pronunciation	Isolated	Final	Medial	Initial
gāf (gold)	......گ......	......گ.....	......گ......	......گ........
	....	....	....	....
	....	....	....	....
	....	....	....	....
	....	....	....	....

Group 12

The only letter in this group is /**lām**/. In its initial and middle positions, it loses its tail.

- Similar to the above letters /kāf/ and /gāf/, its graphic form changes when followed by the non-connector letter /alef/ (see section on Orthographic of connected combinations).

Name & Pronunciation	Isolated	Final	Medial	Initial
lām (lecture)	ل	ـل	ـلـ	لـ

Group 13

This group contains the letter /**mim**/. In its initial and middle positions, it loses its tail.

- Pay attention to the shape of the round head, which must be formed facing downward ad not upward, as often seen in the typeset. The only three letters that have upward rounded head are /fe/qāf/vāv/.

- The letter /mim/ is written in one pen stroke from right to left, head first and then the tail.

Name & Pronunciation	Isolated	Final	Medial	Initial
mim (**m**other)	......ρ........	.......ρ......	.......ـمـ.......	........مـ........
	....	....	....	....
	....	....	....	....
	....	....	....	....
	....	....	....	....

Group 14

This group contains the letter /**nun**/. In its isolated and final positions, this letter is formed under the line, as an open half circle, with one dot placed at the center inside the circle.

- In its initial and medial forms, the half circle is transformed to one tooth followed by a connected short ligature/line, with one dot placed at the center and over the ligature.

- Its appearance is similar to the initial and medial forms of the letters /be, pe, te, se, ye/ (group 2 and 17).

Name & Pronunciation	Isolated	Final	Medial	Initial
nun (nest)	ن	ـن	ـنـ	نـ
ن				

Group 15

This group contains the letter /**vāv**/, which is the last of the seven non-connectors. It may stand for the /v/ sound as well as /o/v/w/.

- In some cases, /vāv/ preceded by the letter /khe/ may be silent (see section on Various Sounds of the Same Letter).

Name & Pronunciation	Isolated	Final	Medial	Initial
vāv (**vote**)	........و........	.......ﻮ.......	.......ﻮ.......	.......ﻭ.......
	....	....	....	....
	....	....	....	....
	....	....	....	....
	....	....	....	....

Group 16

This group contains the letter /**he**/, which appears in various graphic forms as it connects to other letters.

- Only in its isolated position does its form remain unchanged.

- It has a similar sound as the letter /he/ in group 3. However, this /he/ in group 16 may also appear as a silent /he/ like the letter /**h**/ in **h**onor.

Name & Pronunciation	Isolated	Final	Medial	Initial
he (honor)	........ه........	......ـه......	ـهـ /ـه	ـهـ /ـه
	....	....	....	....
	....	....	....	....
	....	....	....	....

Group 17

This group contains the final letter of the alphabet, /**ye**/.

- In its isolated and final forms, it is written in its full form and does not receive any dots.

- In its initial and medial positions, its form is transformed to that of group 2 and 14. It loses its tail and becomes one tooth, followed by a connected short ligature/line with two dots placed at the center and below the ligature. Its appearance is similar to the initial and medial forms of the letters /be/pe/te/se/nun/.

Name & Pronunciation	Isolated	Final	Medial	Initial
ye (yard)	......ی......	....ـی.....	......ـیـ......	..... یـ.....
	....	....	....	....
	....	....	....	....
	....	....	....	....

Vowels

Short vowels

اُ	اِ	اَ
o	**e**	**a**
o as in **orange**; boy	**e** as in **egg**; men	a as in **apple**; jam

The three short vowels (**a, e, o**) are marked above or below the consonant.

- They may be known by their Arabic or Persian names, respectively: /**a**/ (zebar / fatha), /**e**/ (zir / kasra), /**o**/ (pish / zamma).

- They are positioned over or below the letter, which is pronounced before the vowel.

- Short vowels are typically not written; however, in their invisible forms, they are still recognized and thus pronounced.

- In their initial positions, short vowels are supported by /alef/, as a bearer and holder of the vowel, because a short vowel always requires a letter to sit above or below it.

Long vowels

و	ی	ا/آ*
ū	**ī**	**ā**
ū (oo) as in **moon**; pull	ī (ee) as in **kiss**; feel	ā (aa) as in **arm**; far

- Long vowels are visibly recognized as /**ā, ī, ū**/ with elongated sounds, as in /aa, ii, uu/.

- All the initial vowels are supported by an alef / ا / as the bearer.

- The long vowel /ā/ is marked by a hat, like the tilde symbol, placed over alef / آ /. As previously mentioned, the tilde sign is called "maddah" in Arabic, meaning "lengthening" (in Persian, **alef-madd**).

- Only the initial position /ā/ receives the tilde-hat (~), the middle and final positions still are pronounced as a long vowel (ā/aa) but, the hat is no longer marked.

Pronunciation	Isolated	Final	Medial	Initial
ā (ball)	...... ا	.... ل......	...... ل......	...... آ ... ...
آ	....	....	....	....
	....	....	....	....
	....	....	....	....
	....	....	....	....

- In some writings, the madd (~) is placed in the middle of Arabic words where there is a stop after the sound /ā/, such as in:

قُرآن	Qurān (the Islamic holy book)
اِیْدِآل	ideāl (ideal)

- And when the letters alef / ا / and lām / ل / come together, such as in:

| آلآن | alān (just now) |

Diphthongs

Certain consonants and vowels are combined to create certain sounds in Persian: āy, eī/ey, ow, oy, and uy. As you continue with your Persian language studies, you will encounter these sounds in various words.

آی	اِی	اُوْ	اُوْی	اُوی
āy as in **i**ce	eī/ey as in c**a**se	ow as in sh**ow**	oy as in b**oy**	uy as in Spanish m**uy**
چای	نِی	نُوْ	اُوی	جوی
chāy (tea)	ney (reed)	now (new)	oy! (Ahoy!)	juy (stream)

Letters and Vowels Combined

This chart shows the possible positions and forms of the letters as they join with short and long vowels.

- Read and practice from right to left.

Long Vowels			Short Vowels		
و ū	ی ī	ا/آ* ā	اُ o	اِ e	اَ a
بو bū	بی bī	با* bā	بُ bo	بِ be	بَ ba
پو pū	پی pī	پا pā	پُ po	پِ pe	پَ pa
تو tū	تی tī	تا tā	تُ to	تِ te	تَ ta
ثو sū	ثی sī	ثا sā	ثُ so	ثِ se	ثَ sa
جو jū	جی jī	جا jā	جُ jo	جِ je	جَ ja
چو chū	چی chī	چا chā	چُ cho	چِ che	چَ cha
حو hū	حی hī	حا hā	حُ ho	حِ he	حَ ha
خو khū	خی khī	خا khā	خُ kho	خِ khe	خَ kha

دو dū	دی dī	دا dā	دُ do	دِ de	دَ da
ذو zū	ذی zī	ذا zā	ذُ zo	ذِ ze	ذَ za
رو rū	ری rī	را rā	رُ ro	رِ re	رَ ra
زو zū	زی zī	زا zā	زُ zo	زِ ze	زَ za
ژو zhū	ژی zhī	ژا zhā	ژُ zho	ژِ zhe	ژَ zha
سو sū	سی sī	سا sā	سُ so	سِ se	سَ sa
شو shū	شی shī	شا shā	شُ sho	شِ she	شَ sha
صو sū	صی sī	صا sā	صُ so	صِ se	صَ Sa
ضو zū	ضی zī	ضا zā	ضُ zo	ضِ ze	ضَ za
طو tū	طی tī	طا tā	طُ to	طِ te	طَ ta
ظو zū	ظی zī	ظا zā	ظُ zo	ظِ ze	ظَ za
عو ū	عی ī	عا ā	عُ o	عِ e	عَ a
غو qū	غی qī	غا qā	غُ qo	غِ qe	غَ qa

فو fū	فی fī	فا fā	فُ fo	فِ fe	فَ fa
قو qū	قی qī	قا qā	قُ qo	قِ qe	قَ qa
کو kū	کی kī	کا kā	کُ ko	کِ ke	کَ ka
گو gū	گی gī	گا gā	گُ go	گِ ge	گَ ga
لو lū	لی lī	لا lā	لُ lo	لِ le	لَ la
مو mū	می mī	ما mā	مُ mo	مِ me	مَ ma
نو nū	نی nī	نا nā	نُ no	نِ ne	نَ na
هو hū	هی hī	ها hā	هُ ho	هِ he	هَ ha
یو yū	یی yī	یا yā	یُ yo	یِ ye	یَ ya

* Only the initial position /ā/ receives the tilde-hat (~), the middle and final positions (ā) are still pronounced as a long vowel (ā/aa), but the hat is no longer marked.

Note on the short vowels

To further stress the importance of recognizing the positions of the short vowels and memorizing them, note these points:

• These words are often written with invisible short vowels, meaning they are not visibly marked on the word and appear the same.

• Even though they appear the same, they are pronounced differently and have different meanings.

• Example A:

Without visible marking of the short vowels, it appears as ملک, which could be read as any of the pronounciations below with drastically different meanings:

مَلَک	(malak) angel
مَلِک	(malek) king
مِلْک	(melk) property
مُلْک	(molk) kingdom

• Example B:

Without visible marking of the short vowels, it appears as به, void of any specific meaning. However, the same word with marked vowels becomes:

بَه	(bah) goodness
بِه	(beh) quince
بِه	(beh) good
بِه	(be[h], with silent /he/) to

    Tashdid

    Sokun/Jazm

    Hamze

    Alef-maqsure

    Tanvin

    Te-tammat

Signs Chart

Name & Function	Sound	Sign			
Tashdid over the consonant is gemination, doubling of consonant	repetition of the same consonant	ّ			
Sokun or jazm over the consonant is absence of a vowel following the consonant	no sound	ْ			
Hamzeh is glottal stop of the vowel /**a**/ with transliteration symbol /**ʿ**/	stop sound as in **ant**	ء			
		ئ	ؤ	ـؤ	أ
Alef-maqsure, dagger-alef, or reduced alef	ā	ىٰ			
		Isolated ىٰ		Final ـىٰ	
Tanvīn is the final /-**an**/ sound	-an	اً			
Te-tammat (Arabic: Tā-marbūte) marks the final sound /-**t**/ and combined with tanvin marks the final sound /-**tan**/	-t	ة			
		Isolated ة		Final ـة	
	-tan	ةً		ةً	

Tashdid

Name & Function	Sound	Sign
Tashdid over the consonant is gemination, doubling of consonant	repetition of the same consonant	ّ

Tashdid (in Arabic Shaddah) over a letter, in medial and final positions, represents doubled and paired consonants, that is, a consonant repeated twice without any short vowel in between, such as /**nn**/ in "co**nn**ect." In another word, tashdid or gemination is "consonant elongation." A consonant is pronounced for a longer time.

دُکّان | du**kk**ān (shop)

دَرّه | da**rr**e(h) (valley)

- Because in Arabic words the pronunciation of Tashdid determines the meaning of a word, it is important to recognize and retain the Tashdid. In Arabic loan words, any error in the pronunciation of the Tashdid affects the meaning.

- When doubling of consonant occurs in a compound, as the result of two separate words coming together, both similar consonants must be retained, without the use of Tashdid.

پاک کُن | pāk **k**on (eraser)

- A word of caution: in some English transcriptions of the Persian words with two-lettered consonants, such as /**ch**/, /**kh**/, /**zh**/, /**sh**/, /**gh**/ marked by a tashdid, you may find the repeated consonant written only once, for example, "**darreh**" may be written incorrectly as "**dareh**."

Sokun

Name & Function	Sound	Sign
sokun or jazm marking the absent of any vowel following a consonant	no sound	o

Sokun (meaning "silence" in Arabic), also known as jazm, is indicated by a small circle over a consonant that is not followed by a vowel.

- It is not vocalized and marks the absence of a short vowel between two consonants. It connects a consonant directly to the dissimilar following consonant, such as the letters in the English word **st**ood.

مَرْد | **mard** (man)

اَسْب | **asb** (horse)

Hamze[h]

Name & Function	Sound	Sign			
Hamze is a glottal stop representing a hiatus or a stop	Transliterated as ﻋ	ﻋ			
		Alone	Above an un-dotted tooth	Above a vāv	Above or below an alef
		ء	ﺋ	ﺅ	أ

Hamze as a glottal stop /a/ and a hiatus (break, interruption) is carried by /alef/ in combination with short vowels (a, e, o).

إثبات	'esbāt (proof)
أحداث	'ahdās (establishment)
مَبدأ	mabda' (origin)
رأى	ra'i (vote/view)
تأثير	ta'sir (effect)

In all other positions, hamze is carried over the letter /**vāv**/ and over the letter /**ye**/, which in Persian words appears only in the middle of a word as the un-dotted tooth bearer in the above chart, or stands by itself in the final position.

- Hamze written by itself at the end of a word cannot be altered and must be marked.

سؤال	so'āl (question)
آئین	ā'in (ordinance)
اِمضاء	emzā' (signature)

- Hamze, similar to the letter /**eyn**/, has either an apostrophe / ' / or open quotation mark / ' / as its transliteration is sometimes omitted in writing.

- In Persian writing and pronunciation, hamze positioned in the middle of a word may be softened as /ye ی/ such as in:

میگویید ← میگوئید

فایِدِه ← فائِدِه

- Often the Arabic words with hamze are misspelled in Persian for the ease of writing, such as:

Arabic مَسأله	
	mas'le (problem)
Persian مَسئِله	

Alef-maqsure

Name & Function	Sound	Sign	
Alef-maqsure	ā	ىٰ	
		Isolated	Final
		ىٰ	ـىٰ

Alef-maqsure, a reduced long vowel /ā/, is used in some Arabic words, and marked as a final /ye/ with a small vertical /alef/ placed in the center over the /ye/, as in:

موسىٰ	moosā (Moses)
اِلىٰ	elā (up to, until)

- The same /alef/ is also called a dagger-alef, because of its form, and is placed anywhere in an Arabic word. It produces the same /ā/ sound, as in:

اَللّٰه	allāh (God)
اِلٰهى	elāhi (divine)

Tanvin

Name & Function	Sound	Sign
Tanvīn	-an	اً

Tanvin is a sign over the final /alef/ representing the /**an**/ sound often marking an adverb, such as in:

مَعمولاً	maʿmul**an** (usually)
اكثَراً	aksar**an** (mostly)

Te-tammat

Name & Function	Sound	Sign	
Te-tammat (Arabic: Tā-marbūte) marks the final sound /-**t**/ and	-t	ة	
		Isolated ة	Medial/Final ﺔ
combined with tanvin marks the final sound /-**tan**/	-tan	ةً	ﺔً

Te-tammat (in Arabic Tā-marbūte), found at the end of Arabic words, is the coming together of the final /he/ in its silent form, and /te/ which is represented by two dots placed over /he/. It is written as /te/ stacked on top of /he/.

- In some words, tanvin is also added to this combination (**h+t+an**). All three letters are placed on top of one another: two dots represent the sound /t/ placed over /h/ and tanvin /an/ placed over /t/, creating the sound /tan/ (the /h/ remains silent).

This is written as:

كِسوَة	kesvat (garment)
نِعمَة	ne'mat (affluence)
عُمدَةً	'omda**tan** (primarily)
نِسبَةً	nesba**tan** (relatively)

However, in Persian, the writing of the letter /**he** ه/ is eliminated, but the sound is retained and written as –**t** and –**tan**, as in:

کِسوَت	kesvat (garment)
نِعمَت	ne'mat (affluence)
عُمدَتاً	'omda**tan** (primarily)
نِسبَتاً	nesba**tan** (relatively)

Various Sounds of the Same Letter

Letter vāv /و/:

The consonant /vāv و/ is presented in one form, but has multiple sounds:

1)   When it is positioned after a long vowel, it is pronounced /**v**/, as in **v**ote:

v as in vote   باوَر   bāvar (believe)

2)   After a consonant it is pronounced /**o**/, as in m**o**re:

o as in more   خوْردَن   khordan (to eat)

3)   After a sokun sign its sound is elongated /**u**/, as in t**u**ne:

u as in tune   دوْر   dur (far)

4)   After the short vowel /**o**/ it is pronounced /**w**/, as in bo**w**:

w as in bow   لُو   jelow (ahead)

Letter he-havvaz /ه/:

The consonant /he-havvaz/ in its various positions (ه ه ـ ، ـ ه ـ د ـ ه ـ) is phonetically presented as follows:

Real /he/:

When in its initial position and after vowels, it is phonetically aspirated and pronounced with the air forced out of the throat, similar to the letter /h/ in English words "**h**ave" and "**h**allow."

- Except for the word nah (نَه) meaning 'no,' where /he/ is still silent, although it is positioned after a short vowel.

هَوا	**h**avā (air, weather)
هَفت	**h**aft (seven)
هَمیشه	**h**amishe[h] (always)
جَهان	ja**h**ān (world)
کوه	ku**h** (mountain)

Silent /he/:

When /**he**/ is positioned after a consonant, it is no longer aspirated and is pronounced very softly and halfway, as the short vowel /**e**/. For this reason, it is called the silent /he/. It is still written as /he/, but it is pronounced as /e/.

- This is parallel to English where /h/ is not pronounced in some words, for example, **h**onor, **h**our, **h**onest.

بِهْ	be[**h**] (to)
بَچّه	bach.che[**h**] (child)
باغْچِه	bāgh.che[**h**] (small garden)
سِتارِه	setāre[**h**] (star)

Combinations of Cluster Letters

Letters /khe, vāv, alef-madd, ye/

In some cases the letter /khe خ/ coming together with the letter /vāv و/ and followed by the letters /ā آ/ and /ī ی/ only represents the letter /khe/, and the /v/w/ sounds become silent. They have lost their pronunciation due to language changes from Middle Persian to New Persian.

• In Afghanistan, however, some of the /v/w/ sounds are still preserved and pronounced accordingly.

• The list below provides some samples, but keep in mind that /vāv و/ is still written even though it is not pronounced.

1)   /khā/ sound (khe+vāv+alef-madd):

Pronounced ⟵ Written	
خواهَر ⟵ خاهر	Khāhar (sister)
خواب ⟵ خاب	Khāb (sleep)
خواندَن ⟵ خاندَن	Khāndan (to read)
خواهِش ⟵ خاهِش	Khāhesh (request)
خواستَن ⟵ خاستَن	Khāstan (to want)

2) /khī / sound (khe+vāv+ye):

Pronounced ⟵ Written	
خویشتَن ⟵ خیشتَن	Khīshtan (self)
خویشاوَند ⟵ خیشاوَند	Khīshāvand (relative)

Orthographic of connected combinations

Note and practice the different writing for the combinations of letters
/ ā آ / kāf ک / gāf گ / lām ل /:

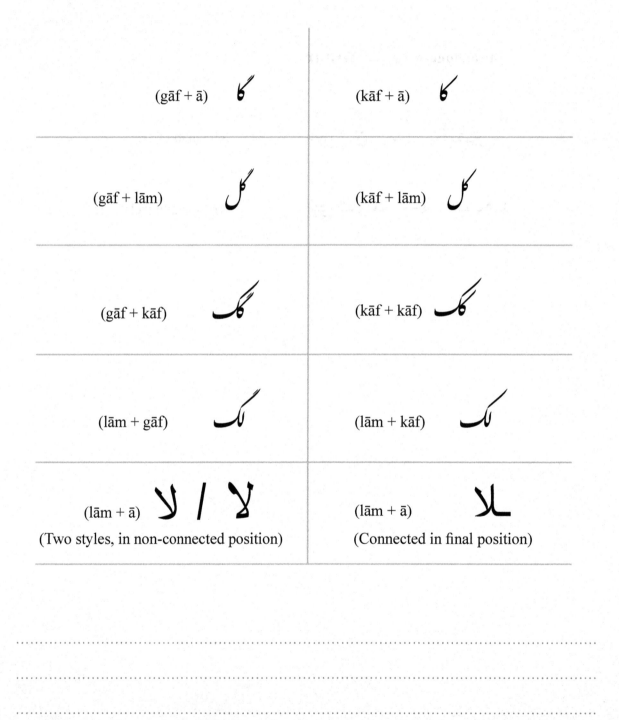

(gāf + ā) گا	(kāf + ā) کا
(gāf + lām) گل	(kāf + lām) کل
(gāf + kāf) گک	(kāf + kāf) کک
(lām + gāf) لگ	(lām + kāf) لک
(lām + ā) لا / لا	(lām + ā) لا
(Two styles, in non-connected position)	(Connected in final position)

....

....

....

....

Cursive Writing & Practice

Translation	Pronunciation	Persian
water	āb	آ + ب = آب ....
		....
		....
		....
		....

Translation	Pronunciation	Persian
father	bābā	ب + ا + ب + ا = بابا ....
		....
		....
		....
		....

Translation	Pronunciation	Persian
bread	nān	ن + ا + ن = نان ....
		....
		....
		....
		....

Translation	Pronunciation	Persian
wind	bād	ب + ا + د = باد ....
		....
		....
		....
		....

Translation	Pronunciation	Persian
bad	bad	بَد = د + َ + ب ....
		....
		....
		....
		....

Translation	Pronunciation	Persian
brother	barādar	بَرادَر = ر + َ + د + ا + ر + َ + ب ....
		....
		....
		....

Translation	Pronunciation	Persian
pomegranate	anār	ا + ذ + ا + ر = اَنار ....
		....
		....
		....
		....

Translation	Pronunciation	Persian
cloud	abr	اَ + بـ + ر = اَبر ....
		....
		....
		....
		....

Translation	Pronunciation	Persian
man	mard	مَرد = د + ْ + ر + َ + م ....
		....
		....
		....
		....

Translation	Pronunciation	Persian
roof	bām	بام = م + ا + ب ....
		....
		....
		....

Translation	Pronunciation	Persian
whistle	sūt	س + ُ + و + ت = سُوت ....
		....
		....
		....
		....

Translation	Pronunciation	Persian
needle	sūzan	س + و + ز + َ + ن = سوزَن ....
		....
		....
		....
		....

Translation	Pronunciation	Persian
(one's) nature	zāt	ذ + ا + ت = ذات ....
		....
		....
		....
		....

Translation	Pronunciation	Persian
child	kudak	ک + و + د + َ + ک = کودَک ....
		....
		....
		....
		....

Translation	Pronunciation	Persian
work; job	kār	ك + ا + ر = كار ....
		....
		....
		....
		....

Translation	Pronunciation	Persian
tray	sīnī	س + ی + ن + ی = سینی ....
		....
		....
		....
		....

Translation	Pronunciation	Persian
sickle	dās	د + ا + س = داس ....
		....
		....
		....
		....

Translation	Pronunciation	Persian
basket	sabad	سَ + َ + بَ + َ + دَ = سَبَد ....
		....
		....
		....
		....

Translation	Pronunciation	Persian
horse	asb	اَ + س + ْ + ب = اَسب ....
		....
		....
		....
		....

Translation	Pronunciation	Persian
apple	sīb	س + ی + ب = سیب ....
		....
		....
		....
		....

Translation	Pronunciation	Persian
snake	mār	مار = ر + ا + م ....
		....
		....
		....
		....

Translation	Pronunciation	Persian
this	īn	این = ن + ی + ا ....
		....
		....
		....

Translation	Pronunciation	Persian
beautiful	zībā	ز + ي + بـ + ا = زيبا ....
		....
		....
		....
		....

Translation	Pronunciation	Persian
wall	dīvār	د + ي + و + ا + ر = ديوار ....
		....
		....
		....
		....

Translation	Pronunciation	Persian
dock	ordak	ا + ُ + د + ر + د + َ + ک = اُردَک ....
		....
		....
		....
		....

Translation	Pronunciation	Persian
goat	boz	ب + ُ + ز = بُز ....
		....
		....
		....
		....

Translation	Pronunciation	Persian
director	modīr	مُدیر = ر + یـ + د + مُ ....
		....
		....
		....
		....

Translation	Pronunciation	Persian
table	mīz	میز = ز + یـ + مـ ....
		....
		....
		....
		....

Translation	Pronunciation	Persian
ball	tup	ت + و + پ = توپ ....
		....
		....
		....
		....

Translation	Pronunciation	Persian
leg	pā	پ + ا = پا ....
		....
		....
		....
		....

Translation	Pronunciation	Persian
old	pīr	پ + ﻴ + ر = پیر ....
		....
		....
		....
		....

Translation	Pronunciation	Persian
soldier	sarbāz	س + ـَ + ر + ب + ا + ز = سَرباز ....
		....
		....
		....
		....

Translation	Pronunciation	Persian
contrary	zed	ضِد = د + ِ + ضـ ....
		....
		....
		....
		....

Translation	Pronunciation	Persian
sharp	tīz	تیز = ز + یـ + تـ ....
		....
		....
		....
		....

Translation	Pronunciation	Persian
rain	bārān	ب + ا + ر + ا + ن = باران ....
		....
		....
		....
		....

Translation	Pronunciation	Persian
sick; patient	bīmār	ب + ی + م + ا + ر = بیمار ....
		....
		....
		....
		....

Translation	Pronunciation	Persian
pigeon	kabūtar	ك + ـَ + بـ + ـَ + تـ + و + بـ + ـَ + رـ = کبوتَر

Translation	Pronunciation	Persian
today	emrūz	ا + ـِ + مـ + ْ + رـ + ْ + و + ُ + ز = اِمروز

Translation	Pronunciation	Persian
scale	tarāzu	ت + َ + ر + ا + ز + و = تَرازو ....
		....
		....
		....
		....
boy	pesar	پ + ِ + س + َ + ر = پِسَر ....
		....
		....
		....
		....

Translation	Pronunciation	Persian
park	pārk	پارک = پ + ا + ر + ْ + ک ....
		....
		....
		....
		....

Translation	Pronunciation	Persian
hand	dast	دَست = ت + س + َ + د ....
		....
		....
		....
		....

Translation	Pronunciation	Persian
berry	tut	.... تـ + و + ت = توت
		....
		....
		....
		....

Translation	Pronunciation	Persian
friend	dūst	.... د + و + سـ + ْ + ـت = دوست
		....
		....
		....
		....

Translation	Pronunciation	Persian
door; inside	dar	دَر = ر + ـَ + د

Translation	Pronunciation	Persian
far	dūr	دور = ر + و + د

Translation	Pronunciation	Persian
bird	parande[h]	پَرَندِه = ه + دِ + نَ + رَ + َ + پَ

Translation	Pronunciation	Persian
book	ketāb	کِتاب = ب + ا + تَ + ِ + کِ

Translation	Pronunciation	Persian
pencil	medād	مِداد = د + ا + د + مِ

Translation	Pronunciation	Persian
breeze	nasīm	نَسیم = م + ی + س + نَ

Translation	Pronunciation	Persian
sky	asemān	آسمان = ن + ا + ه + ِ + س + آ ....
		....
		....
		....
		....

Translation	Pronunciation	Persian
school	madrese[h]	مَدرِسه = ه + ِ + س + ِ + ر + ْ + د + َ + م ....
		....
		....
		....
		....

Translation	Pronunciation	Persian
three	se[h]	سه = ه + ـِ + س
awake	bīdār	بيدار = ر + ا + د + ي + ب

Translation	Pronunciation	Persian
tree	derakht	دِرَخْت = ت + ْ + خ + َ + ر + ِ + د

Translation	Pronunciation	Persian
bed	takht	تَخْت = ت + ْ + خ + َ + ت

Translation	Pronunciation	Persian
nail	mīkh	م + ی + خ = میخ ....
		....
		....
		....
		....

Translation	Pronunciation	Persian
good	khūb	خ + و + ب = خوب ....
		....
		....
		....
		....

Translation	Pronunciation	Persian
house	khāne [h]	خ + ا + ز + ِ + ه = خانه ....
		....
		....
		....
		....

Translation	Pronunciation	Persian
happy	shād	ش + ا + د = شاد ....
		....
		....
		....
		....

Translation	Pronunciation	Persian
dinner	shām	ش + ا + م = شام

behind	posht	پ + ُ + ش + ْ + ت = پُشْت

Translation	Pronunciation	Persian
mosquito	pashe[h]	پَشِه = ه + ِ + شـ + َ + پـ ....
		....
		....
		....
		....

Translation	Pronunciation	Persian
letter	name[h]	نامِه = ه + ِ + مـ + ا + نـ ....
		....
		....
		....
		....

Translation	Pronunciation	Persian
bear	khers	خِرس = س + ر + ِ + خ

Translation	Pronunciation	Persian
rooster	khorūs	خُروس = س + و + ر + ُ + خ

Translation	Pronunciation	Persian
white	sefīd	سِفيد = د + ي + فِ + ِ + س

Translation	Pronunciation	Persian
snow	barf	بَرْف = ف + ْ + ر + َ + ب

Translation	Pronunciation	Persian
trip	safar	سَفَر = ر + ــَ + فـ + ــَ + س

Translation	Pronunciation	Persian
grape	angūr	اَنْگور = ر + و + گ + ْ + ن + اَ

Translation	Pronunciation	Persian
breakfast	sobhāne[h]	صُبحانه = ﻪ + ‌ + ن + ا + ح + ‌ب + ‌ُ + ص ....
		....
		....
		....
		....

bell	zang	زَنْگ = گ + ْ + ن + َ + ز ....
		....
		....
		....
		....

Translation	Pronunciation	Persian
finger	angosht	اَ + ن + گُ + شْ + تْ = اَنْگُشْت ....
		....
		....
		....
		....

Translation	Pronunciation	Persian
one	yek	.... یِ + کْ = یِک
		....
		....
		....
		....

Translation	Pronunciation	Persian
between; among	mīyān	میان = ن + ا + ﻴ + ﻣ ....
		....
		....
		....
		....

Translation	Pronunciation	Persian
shade; shadow	sāye[h]	سایه = ﻪ + ِ + ﻳ + ا + ﺳ ....
		....
		....
		....
		....

Translation	Pronunciation	Persian
visible	peydā	پِیْدا = ا + د + ْ + ـِی + ـَ + پ ....
		....
		....
		....
		....

big	bozorg	بُزُرْگ = گ + ْ + ر + ُ + ز + ُ + بـ ....
		....
		....
		....
		....

Translation	Pronunciation	Persian
spoon	qāshog	ق + ُ + شـ + ا + ق = قاشُق ....
		....
		....
		....
		....

Translation	Pronunciation	Persian
plate	boshqāb	بـ + ُ + شـ + ْ + قـ + ا + ب = بُشْقاب ....
		....
		....
		....
		....

Translation	Pronunciation	Persian
boat	qāyeg	قایِق = ق + یِ + ا + ق ....
		....
		....
		....
		....

Translation	Pronunciation	Persian
room	otāq	اُتاق = ق + ا + ت + اُ ....
		....
		....
		....
		....

Translation	Pronunciation	Persian
sour	torsh	تَ + ُ + ر + ْ + ش = تُرْش ....
		....
		....
		....
		....

salty	shur	شـ + و + ر = شور ....
		....
		....
		....
		....

Translation	Pronunciation	Persian
cat	gorbe[h]	گُرْبِه = ه + ِ + بـ + ْ + ر + ُ + گ ....
		....
		....
		....
		....

wolf	gorg	گُرْگ = گ + ْ + ر + ُ + گ ....
		....
		....
		....
		....

Translation	Pronunciation	Persian
dog	sag	س + ´ + گ = سَگ ....
		....
		....
		....
		....

Translation	Pronunciation	Persian
cow	gāv	گ + ا + و = گاو ....
		....
		....
		....
		....

Translation	Pronunciation	Persian
thread	nakh	نَخ = خِ + َ + نْ ....
		....
		....
		....
		....

Translation	Pronunciation	Persian
chicken	jūje[h]	جوجه = ه + ِ + ج + و + ج ....
		....
		....
		....
		....

Translation	Pronunciation	Persian
crown	tāj	ز + ا + ج = تاج ....
		....
		....
		....
		....

Translation	Pronunciation	Persian
treasure	ganj	گ + ´ + ن + ° + ج = گَنْج ....
		....
		....
		....
		....

Translation	Pronunciation	Persian
rice	berenj	بِرِنْج = ج + ْ + ذ + ِ + ر + ِ + ب ....
		....
		....
		....
		....

banana	mowz	مُوز = ز + و + ُ + م ....
		....
		....
		....
		....

Translation	Pronunciation	Persian
self	khod	خ + و + د = خود ....
		....
		....
		....
		....

Translation	Pronunciation	Persian
meal	khorāk	خ + و + ر + ا + ک = خوراک ....
		....
		....
		....
		....

Translation	Pronunciation	Persian
wheat	gandom	.... گَنْدُم = م + ُ + د + ْ + ن + َ + گ

Translation	Pronunciation	Persian
barley	jow	.... جُو = و + ُ + ج

Translation	Pronunciation	Persian
moonlight	mahtāb	مَهتاب = ب + ا + ت + ه + َ + م ....
		....
		....
		....
		....

star	setāre[h]	سِتاره = ه + ِ + ر + ا + ت + ِ + س ....
		....
		....
		....
		....

Translation	Pronunciation	Persian
all	hame[h]	همه = ه + ِ + م + ِ + ه

every, each	har	هَر = ه + َ + ر

Translation	Pronunciation	Persian
fish	māhī	م + ا + ه + ی = ماهی ....
		....
		....
		....
		....

Translation	Pronunciation	Persian
fox	rubāh	ر + و + ب + ا + ه = روباه ....
		....
		....
		....
		....

Translation	Pronunciation	Persian
north	shomāl	شُمال = ل + ا + مـ + ُ + شـ ....

Translation	Pronunciation	Persian
dress; shirt	pīrāhan	پیراهَن = ن + َ + هـ + ا + ر + یـ + پـ ....

Translation	Pronunciation	Persian
flower	gol	گُل = ل + ُ + گ ....
		....
		....
		....
		....

Translation	Pronunciation	Persian
glass; mug	līvān	لیوان = ن + ا + و + ی + ل ....
		....
		....
		....
		....

Translation	Pronunciation	Persian
tower	borj	بُرْج = ج + ْ + ر + ُ + بـ ....
		....
		....
		....
		....

Translation	Pronunciation	Persian
nest	lāne[h]	لانِه = ه + ِ + ن + ا + لـ ....
		....
		....
		....
		....

Translation	Pronunciation	Persian
sweet	shīrīn	.... ش + یـ + ر + یـ + ن = شیرین
		....
		....
		....
		....

bitter	talkh	.... ت + َ + لـ + ْ + خ = تَلْخ
		....
		....
		....
		....

Translation	Pronunciation	Persian
ear	gush	گ + و + ش = گوش ....
		....
		....
		....
		....

Translation	Pronunciation	Persian
trousers	shalvār	ش + َ + ل + ْ + و + ا + ر = شَلْوار ....
		....
		....
		....
		....

Translation	Pronunciation	Persian
money	pūl	پ + و + ل = پول ....
		....
		....
		....
		....

Translation	Pronunciation	Persian
mushroom	qārch	ق + ا + ر + ٔ + چ = قارچ ....
		....
		....
		....
		....

Translation	Pronunciation	Persian
wood	chūb	چ + ُ + و + ب = چوب ....
		....
		....
		....
		....

Translation	Pronunciation	Persian
chalk	gach	گ + ´ + چ = گَچ ....
		....
		....
		....
		....

Translation	Pronunciation	Persian
wheel	charkh	چَرْخ = خ + ْ + رَ + + چ ....
		....
		....
		....
		....

Translation	Pronunciation	Persian
spring (season)	bahār	بَهار = ر + ا + هَ + + بَ ....
		....
		....
		....
		....

Translation	Pronunciation	Persian
peach	holū	هـ + ُ + ا + و = هُلو ....
		....
		....
		....
		....
jacket	zhākat	ژ + ا + ک + َ + ت = ژاکت ....
		....
		....
		....
		....

Translation	Pronunciation	Persian
eyelash	mozhe[h]	مُژِه = ﻩ + ِ + ژ + ُ + مـ ....
		....
		....
		....
		....

bright	rowshan	رُوْشَن = ن + َ + ش + ْ + و + ُ + ر ....
		....
		....
		....
		....

Translation	Pronunciation	Persian
earth	zamīn	زَمیْن = ن + ْ + یـ + مـ + َ + ز

cup	fenjān	فِنْجَان = ن + ا + ْ + جـ + ـنـ + ِ + ف

Translation	Pronunciation	Persian
elephant	fīl	ف + یـ + ل = فیل ....
		....
		....
		....
		....

Translation	Pronunciation	Persian
sister	kh[w]āhar	خ + و + ا + هـ + َ + ر = خواهَر ....
		....
		....
		....
		....

Translation	Pronunciation	Persian
sleep	kh[w]āb	خ + و + ا + ب = خواب ....
		....
		....
		....
		....

Translation	Pronunciation	Persian
road	jādde[h]	ج + ا + د + ّ + ِ + ه = جادِّه ....
		....
		....
		....
		....

Translation	Pronunciation	Persian
builder (construction)	bannā	بَنّا = ا + ّ + نـ + َ + بـ ....
		....
		....
		....
		....

Translation	Pronunciation	Persian
first	avval	اَوّل = ل + َ + ّ + و + اَ ....
		....
		....
		....
		....

Translation	Pronunciation	Persian
child	bachche[h]	بَچّه = ه + ّ + چ + َ + بِ

soap	sābūn	صابون = ن + و + ْ + بِ + ا + صـ

Translation	Pronunciation	Persian
face	surat	ص + و + ر + ـَ + ت = صورَت

Translation	Pronunciation	Persian
story	dāstān	د + ا + س + ْ + ـَ + ا + ن = داستان

Translation	Pronunciation	Persian
flood	seyl	سِیْل = ل + ْ + یِ + ِ + س ....
		....
		....
		....
		....

Translation	Pronunciation	Persian
tea	chāy	چای = ی + ا + چ ....
		....
		....
		....
		....

Translation	Pronunciation	Persian
time	vagt	وَقْت = ت + ْ + ق + َ + و ....
		....
		....
		....
		....

Translation	Pronunciation	Persian
hello	salām	سَلام = م + ا + ل + َ + س ....
		....
		....
		....
		....

Translation	Pronunciation	Persian
rope	tanāb	طَناب = ب + ا + نـ + َ + ط ....
		....
		....
		....
		....

Translation	Pronunciation	Persian
yard	hayāt	حَیاط = ط + ا + یـ + َ + حـ ....
		....
		....
		....
		....

Translation	Pronunciation	Persian
middle	vasat	و + َ + س + َ + ط = وَسَط ....
		....
		....
		....
		....

Translation	Pronunciation	Persian
candle	sham'	ش + َ + م + ْ + ع = شَمْع ....
		....
		....
		....
		....

Translation	Pronunciation	Persian
friday	jom'e[h]	جُمْعِه = ه + ِ + ع + ْ + م + ُ + ج

Translation	Pronunciation	Persian
bride	'arūs	عَروس = س + و + ُ + ر + َ + ع

Translation	Pronunciation	Persian
hour; clock	sā'at	س + ا + عَ + ت = ساعَت ....
		....
		....
		....
		....

Translation	Pronunciation	Persian
noon	zohr	ظ + ُ + ه + ْ + ر = ظُهْر ....
		....
		....
		....
		....

Translation	Pronunciation	Persian
wealth	servat	ثِروَت = ت + َ + و + ر + ِ + ث ....
		....
		....
		....
		....

Translation	Pronunciation	Persian
inheritance	ers	اِرث = ث + ر + ِ + ا ....
		....
		....
		....
		....

Translation	Pronunciation	Persian
towel	howle[h]	.... حُولِه = ه + ِ + ل + و + ُ + ح
		....
		....
		....
		....

morning	sobh	.... صُبْح = ح + ْ + ب + ُ + ص
		....
		....
		....
		....

Translation	Pronunciation	Persian
bath	hammām	حَمّام = م + ا + ّ + ﻤ + َ + ﺤ

Translation	Pronunciation	Persian
dew	jāle[h]	ژاله = ﻪ + ِ + ل + ا + ژ

Translation	Pronunciation	Persian
sunset	qorūb	غُروب = ب + و + ُ + ر + ُ + غ ....
		....
		....
		....
		....

Translation	Pronunciation	Persian
sorrow	qosse[h]	غُصّه = ه + ِ + ّ + ص + ُ + غ ....
		....
		....
		....
		....

Translation	Pronunciation	Persian
season; chapter	fasl	فَصْل = ل + ْ + ص + َ + ف

Translation	Pronunciation	Persian
pool	estakhr	اِسْتَخْر = ر + ْ + خ + َ + ت + ْ + س + ِ + ا

Translation	Pronunciation	Persian
tired	khaste[h]	خَسْته = ه + ِ + تَ + ْ + س + َ + خ
		....
		....
		....
		....

sun	khorshīd	خورْشید = د + ی + ش + ْ + ر + و + خ
		....
		....
		....
		....

Translation	Pronunciation	Persian
mind	zehn	ذ + ِ + هـ + ن = ذِهن ....
		....
		....
		....
		....

Translation	Pronunciation	Persian
feather	par	پ + َ + ر = پَر ....
		....
		....
		....
		....

Translation	Pronunciation	Persian
forest	jangal	جَنْگَل = ل + َ + گَ + ْ + نَ + َ + ج
		....
		....
		....
		....

Translation	Pronunciation	Persian
bravo!	āfarin	آفَرین = ن + ی + ر + َ + ف + آ
		....
		....
		....
		....

Transformation of Naskh to Nasta'liq

In Naskh, letters in their different positions (isolated, initial, medial, and final) are written in two shapes only: joined, and isolated/non-joined. However, in the Nasta'liq style, some of the letters can be written differently when joined to another letter. Letters are uniformly written on the line in Naskh, but they are written in cascading form in the Nasta'liq, and often formed according to the personal taste of the writer, similar to a drawing.

Examples of Naskh and Nasta'liq are provided here, showing the transformation from one style to another, both in typed and handwritten form:

Dots:

In the Nast 'liq style of writing, the formation of dots becomes more relaxed.

- The one dot is still written in the same form, the two dots centered below and centered above a letter would each transform to a hyphen (-).

- The three dots are transformed either as a small half circle, or a hyphen with one dot placed above it, if it is positioned above a letter (as in /she/), and a hyphen with one dot placed below it, if it is positioned below a letter (as in /pe/).

Handwritten Nasta'liq	Typed Nasta'liq	Naskh
یمیشہ/ہمیشہ	ہمیشہ	هَمیشه
مہتاب	مہتاب	مَهتاب
چشم	چشم	چَشم
پست	پست	پُست
ایران	ایران	ایران

Letters /re, ze, zhe, mim, ye/:

In the Nasta'liq style of writing, when more than one tooth precede the letters / re, ze, zhe, mim, ye / then the final tooth changes its form and becomes a hump before attaching itself to the aforementioned letters.

Handwritten Nasta'liq	Typed Nasta'liq	Naskh
پیر	پیر	پیر
میز	میز	میز
منیژه	منیژه	مَنیژه
نیم	نیم	نیم
بینی	بینی	بینی

....

....

....

....

....

....

Letter /nun/:

However, the letter /nun/ always connects itself directly after the preceding tooth, and no change is made to its preceding tooth (no hump).

Handwritten Nasta'liq	Typed Nasta'liq	Naskh
این	این	این
جشن	جشن	جَشن
چین	چین	چین
سیمین	سیمین	سیمین
آبتین	آبتین	آبتین

....

....

....

....

....

....

....

Letters /jim, che, he, khe/:

In the Nasta'liq style of writing, the letters /jim, che, he, khe/ in their middle and final positions, referenced as the "descenders," change their form and are positioned stacked in a cascading position.

Handwritten Nasta'liq	Typed Nasta'liq	Naskh
حجم	حجم	حَجم
بچّہ	بچّہ	بَچّہ
صلح	صلح	صُلح
محجوب	محجوب	مَحجوب
پُختَن	پختن	پُختَن

....

....

....

....

....

....

• When more than one letter precedes letters /jim, che, he, khe/, then the final tooth changes its form and becoes a hump before attaching itslf to the mentioned letters.

Handwritten Nasta'liq	Typed Nasta'liq	Naskh
پنج	پنج	پَنج
گنج	گنج	گَنج
پیچ	پیچ	پیچ
منحنی	منحنی	مُنحَنی
مشخص	مشخص	مُشَخَّص

Letters /sin, shin/:

In the Nasta'liq style of writing, teeth in the letters **/sin, shin/** are transformed to an elongated ligature.

Handwritten Nasta'liq	Typed Nasta'liq	Naskh
پست	پت	پُست
سیستان	سیتان	سیستان
شیر	شیر	شیر
گنجشک	گنجشک	گُنجِشک
شیراز	شیراز	شیراز

....

....

....

....

....

....

....

....

- However, when a combination of these two letters /**sin, shin**/ are written together, without any letter in between, then only one letter can be elongated, and the other would remain in its original form.

Handwritten Nasta'liq	Typed Nasta'liq	Naskh
شِش	شِش	شِش
شُستَن	شُتن	شُستَن
سُت	ست	سُت
سِشوار	سِشوار	سِشوار
نِشُستَن	نِشتن	نِشَستَن

....

....

....

....

....

....

....

....

Letter /he/:

In the Nast'liq style of writing, the initial, middle, and final /he/ change their forms (also see Group 16).

Handwritten Nasta'liq	Typed Nasta'liq	Naskh
هر / هر	هر	هَر
همه / همه	همه	هَمه
مهتاب	مهتاب	مَهتاب
همهمه / همهمه	همهمه	هَمهَمِه
جهان	جهان	جَهان

....

....

....

....

....

....

....

....

Days of the Week

In Afghanistan and Iran Saturday is the first day of the week, and Friday is the final day.

English	Pronunciation	Persian
Saturday	shanbe[h]	شَنْبِه
Sunday	yek.shanbe[h]	يِكْشَنْبِه
Monday	do.shanbe[h]	دوشَنْبِه
Tuesday	se.shanbe[h]	سِه شَنْبِه
Wednesday	chahār.shanbe[h]	چَهارشَنْبِه
Thursday	panj.shanbe[h]	پَنْج شَنْبِه
Friday	jom'e[h]	جُمْعِه

Seasons

In Afghanistan and Iran the official Calendar begins with the first day of Spring.

English	Pronunciation	Persian
Spring	bahār	بَهار
Summer	tābestān	تابِسْتان
Fall	pāīz	پاییز
Winter	zemestān	زِمِسْتان

Months of the Calendar

Spring بَهار (bahār)

English	Pronunciation	Persian
21 March-20 April	farvardīn (31 days)	فَرْوَرْدین
21 April-21 May	ordībehesht (31 days)	اُرْدیبِهِشْت
22 May-21 June	khordād	خُرْداد

Summer تابِسْتان (tābestān)

English	Pronunciation	Persian
22 June-22 July	tīr (31 days)	تیر
23 July-22 Aug.	mordād (31 days)	مُرْداد
23 Aug.-22 Sept.	shahrīvar (31 days)	شَهْریوَر

Fall پاییز **(pāīz)**

English	Pronunciation	Persian
23 Sept.-22 Oct.	mehr (30 days)	مِهْر
23 Oct.-21 Nov.	ābān (30 days)	آبان
22 Nov.-21 Dec.	āzar (30 days)	آذَر

Winter زِمِسْتان **(zemestān)**

English	Pronunciation	Persian
22 Dec.-19 Jan.	dey (30 days)	دِیْ
20 Jan.-18 Feb.	bahman (30 days)	بَهْمَن
19 Feb.-20 March	esfand (30 days)	اِسْفَنْد

Numbers

The cardinal numbers, following their Hindu (Indian) numeric origin, are written from left to right, similar to English: 0 (zero), 1 (one), 2 (two), 3 (three), 4 (four), 5 (five), 6 (six), 7 (seven), 8 (eight), 9 (nine), 10 (ten).

Numeral in Persian	Name in Persian	Pronunciation	Number
.	صِفْر	sefr	0
١	یِک	yek	1
٢	دو	du	2
٣	سِه	se[h]	3
۴ / ٤*	چَهار	chahār (chār)**	4
۵ / ٥*	پَنْج	panj	5
۶ / ٦*	شِش	shesh (shish)**	6
٧	هَفْت	haft	7
٨	هَشْت	hasht	8
٩	نُه	noh	9
١.	دَه	dah	10

* As written in Arabic

** Colloquial pronunciation

Numeral in Persian	Name in Persian	Pronunciation	Number
۱۱	یازدَه	yāz.dah	11
۱۲	دَوازدَه	davāz.dah	12
۱۳	سیزدَه	sīz.dah	13
۱۴	چَهاردَه	chahār.dah	14
۱۵	پانْزدَه	pānz.dah	15
۱۶	شانْزدَه	shānz.dah	16
۱۷	هِفْدَه	hef.dah	17
۱۸	هِجْدَه	hej.dah	18
۱۹	نوزْدَه	nūz.dah	19
۲۰	بیسْت	bīst	20

* After number 20, the numbers folowing are formed in a comination of 20 plus the connecting word "and" which here is pronounced as 'o' and then the following number.

• For example, number 21 is formed as bist-o-yek (20 and 1), 22 is bist-o-du (20 and 2), and 35 is si-o-panj (30 and 5).

Numeral in Persian	Name in Persian	Pronunciation	Number
۲۱	بیست و یک*	bīst-o-yek	21
۳۰	سی	sī	30
۴۰	چِهِل	chehel	40
۵۰	پَنْجاه	panjāh	50
۶۰	شَصْت	shast	60
۷۰	هَفْتاد	haftād	70
۸۰	هَشْتاد	hashtād	80
۹۰	نَوَد	navad	90

- 101 is sad-o-yet (100 and 1), 1001 is hezar-o-yek (1000 and 1), and continues in the same manner in every tens, hundreds, and thousands series.

Numeral in Persian	Name in Persian	Pronunciation	Number
١٠٠	صَد	sad	100
٢٠٠	دِویسْت	devīst	200
٣٠٠	سیصَد	sī.sad	300
٤٠٠	چَهارْصَد	chahār.sad	400
٥٠٠	پانْصَد	pān.sad	500
٦٠٠	شِشْصَد	shesh.sad	600
٧٠٠	هَفْتْصَد	haft.sad	700
٨٠٠	هَشْتْصَد	hasht.sad	800
٩٠٠	نُهْصَد	noh.sad	900
١,٠٠٠	هِزار	hezār	1,000
١,٠٠٠,٠٠٠	مِلْیون	melyūn	1,000,000
١,٠٠٠,٠٠٠,٠٠٠	میلْیارْد	milliard	1,000,000,000

CPSIA information can be obtained
at www.ICGtesting.com
Printed in the USA
LVOW04s1702070318
568997LV00010B/483/P